OUT

 *of the*

ASHES

I Rise

Ernestine Walkes

ISBN 978-1-0980-1100-0 (paperback)
ISBN 978-1-0980-1101-7 (digital)

Christian Faith Publishing, Inc.
832 Park Avenue
Meadville, PA 16335
www.christianfaithpublishing.com

All names have been changed to protect everyone.

Printed in the United States of America

This book is a tribute to evangelist and prophetess Mrs. Florence Clementina Waterman (deceased) my mother, Charleen Richardson-Walkes (daughter), Charles Walkes (son), Rudolf Waterman (deceased), adopted parents Edgar and Euna Dawson, and Olivere St. Cox (former headmaster).

MY JOURNEY

As I awoke on May 25, 1965, I inhaled a breath of fresh air while observing the sun peeking through the clouds above the horizon. The various colors of orange, yellow, and white captured my attention as the light white clouds whisked across the sky.

The day I anxiously awaited had finally arrived, hopefully setting the stage for my career advancement and a world of opportunities. Of course, I was excited because due to economic conditions which resulted in a low cash flow since the death of the head of household, my father (Westerman Waterman) who had passed away at the tender age of forty-seven years old leaving behind a young wife (Florence C. Waterman), forty-two years old a mother of eight children (six boys and two girls) to be taken care of, ranging from twenty-six years to four years old of which I'm the last of sixteen siblings; eight children survived.

My parents seriously believed in God's injunction of "love" from Genesis 1:25 which says, "Be fruitful and multiply," considering back in that era, modes of entertainment were limited that they heartedly agreed to fulfill the command of love. I always wonder if my dad died with a smile on his face. At the age of four years old, I was too young to comprehend what was going on.

Someone said, "Life is a journey." With the journey comes mountains and valleys, roadblocks and detours as we navigate through life's pathway. Another statement I draw strength from is, "Life is like a deck of cards." Sometimes, we're fortunate to get a good hand. Whatever the case is ultimately, we make the best of what we're given. Radio host Steve Harvey once said, "10 percent is what is given to you, and 90 percent is how you deal with the remaining cards in the deck." In retrospect, I'm truly grateful to God for the experiences I've encountered along life's pathway.

You ask me why?

I'm glad you asked. It made me a stronger person of faith enabling me to become the strong woman of character which I've grown up to be. I have a great appreciation for life which is attributed to the foundation laid by my mum (Florence Waterman) who transcended January 9, 2006 at the age of ninety-six years old succumbing to diabetes—what a phenomenal woman. Having a positive attitude and great faith mitigates half of the problem being solved because you can't develop into all that you want to be if you continue to hold on to the past. "Casting all our cares upon him for he careth for us."

My mum, Florence Clementina Jordan-Waterman, was a matriarch and disciplinarian, a great trooper, and a phenomenal woman who never compromises her values or morals. Being a spiritual, God-fearing woman, she started every morning with hours of prayers namely for the following:

1. Family
2. Government worldwide that God Almighty would enable the government body to make the right decisions on behalf of the various countries

She believed God was the only potentate who ordained all earthly leadership. As a young girl growing up, I observed her reading the Bible daily, committing many portions of the Bible to memory. Some of her favorite passages of scripture were found in Proverbs 13:24 (KJV) which says, "He that spareth the rod hateth his son, but he that loveth him chasteneth him betimes" and in Proverbs 29:15 which says, "The rod and reproof gives wisdom, but a child left to himself bringeth his mother to shame."

She was a hard-working, domesticated, spiritual woman who hustle planting vegetables and ground provisions both to buy and sell. She wore many hats, mastering most of them—kudos to her. The skills she acquired enabled her to meet her family needs like paying bills and keeping a roof over our heads. Being a proud but humble woman, she never settled for less. She laid a strong foundation for her family of which I'm proud to say has been instrumental in my career development.

All of her children are career achievers including two Bishops. She's the first single mother in the island of Barbados to be bless with such accomplishments. It amazes me when I hear people say, "Mothers can't raise boys," whether this statement is coming from the media or jester as a general statement. Usually, when boys go astray becoming part of statistics, the focus of the blame targets an absentee father. Nonsense, yes! It's important that children of both sexes would benefit from the knowledge and experiences shared by both parents of the opposite sex which would enable them later on in life when confronted with major decisions. One doesn't wait until the horse gets out of the stable to chase after it; you discipline the horse, taking absolute control while securing its dwelling.

Yes! In the twentieth century children have more "rights" given to them by the government, reason why respect is at its lowest level.

Unfortunately, the jails are full of juveniles and adults. Those of us who have been bless with children need to set ground rules, respect being the number one priority. As the saying goes, "Home drum beats first," if we as parents fail to delegate setting a solid foundation for our children to build on as they mature into adulthood, we can't blame society for our lack of leadership. As the saying goes, "If we fail to plan, we plan to fail." Therefore, be prepared to live with the consequences.

Mum's motto was based on biblical concepts like Proverbs 13:24 (KJV) which says, "He that spareth his rod hateth his son: but he that chasteneth him betimes." Another of her quotations is found in book of Proverbs 29:15 (KJV) which says, "The rod and reproof gives wisdom; but a child left to himself bringeth his mother to shame."

In the twentieth century, many people sarcastically asked, "Where was Agency for Child Services [ACS]?" If the government agency had existed during that era, 95 percent of our parents would have been incarcerated because of the disciplinary actions they implemented. Mum's system of raising children seemed regimental, but it worked resulting in raising eight professional children who never had an encounter with the law, except for marriage or natural death.

Kudos to my mum who was a hard-working, spiritual, domesticated woman who hustle planting vegetables, buying and selling products, baking, cooking, etc., whatever deemed necessary to feed her family, to pay bills, and to keep a roof over her family's heads.

I recall one day, Mum requested one of my nephews to pick a branch of water coconuts before we left for primary school. She noticed one of the coconuts had burst when it hit the ground. Before she could notify my nephew that she was going under the tree to retrieve the coconut, another coconut fell from the branch striking her head. In horror, my nephews and I watched as the blood stream from her nostrils and mouth. She started to pray asking God for divine guidance and aid as she laid on the ground trying to compose herself. We cried not knowing what impact the injury would lead to.

However, when she regained consciousness, she told us, "It's all right. Go on to school. God would take care of me."

Yes! God did. The Bible states, "Call on him and he'll answer." Mum had a great faith. Thank God, Mum lived to reach the golden age of ninety-six years. Fifty years after the incident, she never suffered any form of brain damage or dementia. Praise God.

Mum was a praying woman who prayed for hours, praying for her family and the government worldwide as a whole. She believed God alone was the only potentate and that he ordained all earthly leadership. She read the Bible daily and committed to memorize large portions of the scriptures. She also "pray and fast" every Wednesday. This labor of love continued into her late eighties until her diabetic condition virtually made it impossible to continue her love quest weekly regime.

Ultimately, diabetes was the leading cause of her demise at the age of ninety-six years old.

CARING

Mum believed in and applied the simplicity and practicability of the Gospels, catering for the physical, emotional, and spiritual needs of all people. She provided nutritious meals for our families as well as for the sick and shut-in. These errands were carried out by her last two children and grandchildren.

From the late 1950s through the early 1960s, Mum would prepare and send meals to homebound, bedridden people in the neighborhood whose health was impaired with diseases as well as those people who suffered with strokes. Mum migrated to the United States in 1968 and traveled to England in 1972. However, upon her return to Barbados in 1981, she continued to provide meals for 2 of her brothers who lived beyond 100 years old. One brother lived to be 105 years old.

Mum wasn't rich. But like the widow in 1 Kings 17:8 who only had enough meal to feed herself and her son because she obeyed the prophet Elijah who requested to be fed first then she could feed herself and her son, God multiplied her food supply. Philippians 2:3 says, "Do nothing from selfishness or concert, but in humility count others better than yourself." Let each of you look not only to your own interest but also to the interest of others. When preparing to cook for a meal, she always added extra in preparation for unannounced families or strangers who stopped by.

I also witness that if the family was eating and someone showed up unexpectedly, my mum was contented giving her food away as she settled to eat a slice of bread and a cup of tea. She was a good Samaritan.

RESPECT

Spare not the rod and spoil the child.

—Proverbs 13:24 (KJV)

She raised her children and grandchildren in the fear and reverence of the Lord, always applying biblical principles as the ultimate criteria for our conduct. We were taught to obey and respect our elders, teachers, as well as those individuals who were given authority over us. The Proverbs 22:6 (KJV) states, "Train up a child in the way it should grow, and when he's/she's old, he/she will not depart from it."

I personally think that if these rules were implemented today, twentieth-century era, we as a society would experience a low crime rate. I'm quite please to read in the *New York Daily News* April 2018 issue that the state of Kentucky is allowing Scripture in schools as part of their studies.

EDUCATION

Mum was an avid reader, reading hundreds of books, retaining childhood poems which she recited yearly at "Sunday school programs." She prepared her children and grandchildren for primary school by teaching us penmanship as she drew additional lines in our notebooks while guiding our fingers as we wrote the alphabet, numbers, and letters in between the original book lines as well as the new lines she created. As time went by, she taught us basic mathematics, the concepts of adding figures, subtraction, multiplication, decimals, measurements, as well as various tables listed at the back of the notebook. In addition to mathematics and English, we were given words from a third-grade English book to find the meanings from the *Collins English Dictionary* and followed by making sentences with the words, building our vocabulary since people judge a person by the way they speak. Back in those days, speaking proper English was very important.

She believed in order to be competitive and to excel in life, one should have a good academic foundation in mathematics and the English language. During our junior high school years, my siblings and I received private tutoring from the neighborhood teachers to become more proficient and competitive in our studies. In addition to being academically inclined, she believed everyone should learn a trade/profession as a backup in the event we encountered a roadblock during our journey through life. Being versatile would be a plus on our résumé. One should always be prepared for the unexpected, being able to navigate through life with minimum interruption.

During the 1950s, she single-handedly started Sunday school at Hillaby Christian Mission Church with four children. Subsequently, the neighbor's children joined the Sunday school classes which grew tremendously, forcing Mum to seek assistance from some of the older adults which she trained at church to assist her in her quest to educate the Sunday school children. Due to the large increase in attendance, the classes were divided into three division namely as follows:

1. Infant children from three to five years old
2. Young people from six to fifteen years old
3. Adults

At the end of classes, everyone was expected to participate in reciting a Bible verse, especially the golden rule, "Do unto others as you would like them to do unto you."

Yes! Respect which is lacking in the "twentieth century." The young people and adults were required to memorize the Bible verses in addition to reading a chapter per week. She set an example for others to follow by reciting recitations during Easter and Christmas program celebrations along with the Sunday school children. Her favorite poem was titled "Honor to Christ."

At the end of the programs, the children received a bag of roasted peanuts and candies.

My mum (Florence Waterman) was the last of twelve children born to Mary-Ann Drakes and Joseph Jordan—eight boys and four girls. She accepted Jesus Christ at the tender age of seven. In 1925, she married Westerman Waterman. That union produced sixteen children of which eight survived—six boys and two girls.

MEDICAL FIELD

I witnessed Mum applying the practicability of the Gospel as she catered to the needs of people spiritually, physically, and emotionally. I'll share a few scenarios with you.

David, our neighbor, whose ankle was punctured with a twig as he walked through grass field ignored the injury until it became enflamed and pain was fully affecting his ability to walk. The wound progressively grew worse as the flesh became indented. Mum applied antiseptic, cleaning the wound thoroughly. She applied the inside of white bread mixed with castor oil, prayed and believed in God to heal the infected foot. The wound miraculously was healed. David lived past ninety years of age.

Another occasion was when a man had a growth on his back which was known as a carbuncle. Mum prayed to God and sterilized the area as she used a large razor, lancing the area around the growth, applying pressure as the inflammation oozed out. A ball-like tissue exited which she stated was the root. Every day, she cleaned the wound applying home remedies until the wound was completely healed.

One of my schoolmates fell while playing dislocating her shoulder. As my girlfriend screamed in pain, Mum placed her to lie down as she prayed applying pressure on the shoulder blade jerking the arm into the socket. Miraculously, it healed without complications.

Mum was one of the neighborhood nurses who attended patients with cuts on their fingers, limbs, etc. She assisted midwives in the delivery of babies based on her God-given skills.

She counseled youngsters whose parents deemed them hopeless cases because their actions and poor judgment resulted in incarceration. She also counseled unwed mothers who she embraced applying biblical principles, caring for them and giving them hope. She administered hope to the hopeless.

There was a case wherein one of her sisters passed away leaving a young baby boy who was breastfed. Mum had given birth around the same time her sister had a baby and opted to breastfeed her nephew.

A phenomenal woman.

DEVOTION

I recalled as a child growing up in my home, the first order of the day begun with prayer as well as "prayer and fast" every Wednesday. This labor of love continued into her late 1980s when she was diagnosed with diabetes, which progressively grew worst making it impossible to continue her weekly prayer regime.

My younger brother, who's two years my junior, my two nephews, and I started the day with family worship. Our older siblings migrated overseas. The oldest brother relocated to the USA while my sister and five brothers migrated to London, United Kingdom. My siblings and I were required to kneel while everyone repeated the Lord's Prayer individually. As time went by, we incorporated more praise (e.g., praying for friends, family, love ones, the poor, needy, sick, and afflicted).

The government (those set-in authority over us) seeking God's guidance which would enabled them to make the right decisions on behalf of the citizens worldwide. The final prayer incorporated praying for people in the medical field (doctors, nurses, scientist, etc.) that God would provide them wisdom to do only what is necessary during and after surgery, administering tender, loving care (TLC) as needed.

At the end of devotion, we were given a nice breakfast as we prepared to go off to school. On our return home from school, a healthy dinner awaited us. Mum believed no one could function effectively if they were hungry. It was the vehicle to being able to concentrate on the academic subjects being taught. No one can fully comprehend what is being taught when they're hungry.

My mother's mother, Mary-Ann Drakes-Jordan, passed away when I was around seven years of age. I had a deep feeling that if I was a nurse, I would been able to administer the necessary tender, loving care (TLC) needed which would had enabled her to live longer. Little did I know that "life's a journey," and at her golden age of ninety plus, she had completed her mission here on earth. I expressed my desire to pursue a nursing career to my mum, who motivated me to apply to the various hospitals in United Kingdom (London, England). Finally, after several petitions to the various hospitals, I was accepted by the Rush Green Hospital in London where I had submitted measurement for my nursing uniforms as I prepared to embark on my vision.

My eldest brother, Vincent, visited Barbados for the first time in December 1964 after leaving the island during the 1930s. When he first saw me, he was ecstatic learning of my academic accomplishment—a five-year scholarship to Federal High School under the leadership of Mr. Joy Edwards, the principal (deceased). Moving on to the Metropolitan High School under the leadership of Mr. Olivere St. Cox, who was a motivating factor in my academic development. He also believed in "spare not the rod and spoil the child." If you failed to prepare your homework thoroughly for as many as five subjects, he always walks around with a belt or twig to administer punishment. I always had an excuse.

I told him, "It was that time of the month." Therefore, if he whip me, I could have a hemorrhage and die. Weeks later, he would approach me stating, "Are you still cycling?" As I began to run, he would catch me with the tip of the belt or twig. Those were the days when teachers had children's best interest at heart. There was a great amount of respect for teachers, guardians, and our elder adults.

Upon returning to New York, my brother Vincent's wife (Elaine Coulthurst Waterman) passed away on Easter Sunday 1965. My brother convinced Mum to send me to New York instead of England where two of my uncle's daughters had completed their nursing studies at Brooklyn Jewish Hospital. One daughter being an RN (registered nurse) and another daughter being a nursing administrator at Brooklyn Jewish Hospital.

Our mum thought it was wise to send me to New York to study as well as aiding with my brother raising his seven-year-old daughter while pursuing my dream of becoming a registered nurse. One must always be prepared for the journey which lies ahead.

Yes!

There would be mountains and valleys but because Christ overcame we as followers who emulate him, we too must exercise our faith in him knowing that "if he brings us to it, he'll bring us through it." Isaiah 43:2 states, "When we walk through the water, he'll be with us through the rivers they wouldn't over flow us: when we walk through the fire we shall not burn, neither shall the flame kindle upon us."

Upon arriving at JFK (John Fitzgerald International Airport), I was greeted by family members who showered me with love, hugs, and kisses—a royal welcome. Everyone was delighted to see me. As the car maneuvered along the highways, the scenery was breathtaking (e.g., beautiful skylines, tall and massive buildings, and gorgeous landscaping). At the tender age of sixteen years old, I wondered if that was a dream as I looked for the street which I was led to believe was paved with gold—America, the land of opportunity. The sky is the limit. President John Kennedy stated, "Ask not what your country can do for you, but what you can do for the country." A statement which always resonated in my brain.

I set up residence in Midtown Manhattan with my oldest brother, Reverend Vincent M. Waterman, who had migrated to New York during the early 1930s seeking employment and furthering his education. We were strangers to each other but still siblings—he being the first of our parents' children and I being the last of the surviving eight children. He was the first of our siblings to travel abroad, and I was the last of the siblings traveling abroad, both of us coincidently living in USA.

Most of my relatives lived in Brooklyn, a few lived in the boroughs of Manhattan and the Bronx although scattered throughout the boroughs. Distances didn't keep us apart; we were an inseparable family. As the saying goes, "United we stand, divided we fall." As the sayings goes, "A family that prays together, stays together." My time was split amongst the families. However, since one of my favorite uncle's children in Brooklyn was around my age, I looked forward worshipping with that family on Sundays at the Eben-Ezer Christian Mission Church in Bedford-Stuyvesant now known as Stuyvesant Heights. I was active in the choir, traveling to the various churches within the metropolitan area as well as out of state.

My father's family who lived in Manhattan and the Bronx was materialistic and worldly. Let's keep it real. To be able to well balance during our journey through life, one should be versatile, well balance and knowledgeable during our journey through life being exposed to good and evil, both side of life, which I gracefully embraced since life experiences equips us with the knowledge and experience. My aunts catered to my worldly needs like buying me jewelry; pampering me; showering me with clothing, the latest hairstyle, and entertainment including boat rides especially around Manhattan skyline; and teaching me the latest dances, which was a "no-no" when I was growing up as a child in Barbados, West Indies. I embraced all the attention every teenager craves.

Growing up, we weren't allowed to dance, play dominoes, listen to calypso music, nor read comics books. Thank God for America, I was exposed to both sides of the world. Although Mum was overprotective, shielding her children from the vices of the world, she taught us that "there's something good in the worst of us and something bad in the best of us." Therefore, think before you speak because spoken words cannot be erased. If you have nothing good to say about someone, don't say anything because it could be damaging to someone's character.

I read a story once wherein someone was accused of a crime which escalated to trial in the court of law. The judge questioned the witness who retracted his false statement, but the victim's character was already damaged. The judge told the false witness before handing down sentencing of punishment toward him. He requested him to complete a task. He was instructed to tear up a piece of paper into several small pieces and to throw them out of the car as he travels home. He was ordered to return back to court the following day for sentencing.

When the case was called, the judge told the false witness that he wanted him to return to the area where he dispose the paper and bring it back to the court.

The false witness stated, "It would be impossible to retrieve all the papers since the wind blew most of it away."

Before dismissing the case, the judge told the false witness that he hoped he learned his lesson of defamation of one's character flies all over just like the bits of paper. Be careful how you treat people in the future.

As the novelty wore off, it was time to begin my studies which began at Rhoades Preparatory School and moving on to Washington Irvington Evening High School, graduating in 1967 with a high school diploma. I enrolled at the Metropolitan School of Infant and Geriatric Care in Manhattan, New York, graduating with a certificate in 1969. Having a quest for knowledge, I attended classes at St. Francis College and Medgar Evers College, graduating in 1988 in BSc in management, minor in marketing. My vision to become a registered nurse was placed on the back burner because of a low cash flow.

My brother informed me that he was operating on a low budget since the passing of his wife, who was an asthmatic and was constantly in and out of the hospital. He couldn't afford to send me to a nursing school. If he had conveyed this information to Mum, I would have pursued my studies in United Kingdom (London). However, he assured me that our uncle and his children would assist me in my quest to pursue a career in the nursing field. I later learned that this was the beginning of my brother stretching the truth. Our uncle was barely surviving; however, with the supplemental aid of his children, he was able to keep his head above the water.

My brother Reverend Vincent Milyard Waterman (African Orthodox Church) made my life a living *hell*. I experienced a chaotic journey living at his residence being subjected to violation and abuse.

I landed my first job at Bear Stearns & Co. 1 Wall Street, N.Y., at First Wall Street, New York, with a starting pay of $95.00 per week working in the PS (purchasing and sales) department in 1967–1972. Vincent demanded for my paycheck.

I bluntly told him, "No way." I earned this check. Therefore, I agreed to pay $10.00 toward food, $10.00 for rent, and $10.00 toward the telephone which I was limited to five minutes per day since he would be expecting calls from Washington, which never materialized during the three years I lived at his premises located at 875 Amsterdam Avenue, New York. The rent was only $75.00 per month from May 23, 1965 through October 4, 1968.

One day, he instructed me to place his name on all of my documents making him the beneficiary because if anything should happen to me, Mum would have difficulty obtaining any money from the various institutions. Also, it would take her four hours by airplane from Barbados to the USA, provided the USA immigration granted her entry.

I ignored everything he said, leaving my assets to Mum. My actions added to his infuriation. He became more infuriated because I paid the rent with a check. He stated that I was following the advice of our Barbadian neighbors (Dawson), who he had introduced me to. I bonded with their daughter who was one year older than me. Their daughter and I bonded well. Later, she became my daughter's godmother.

Their home in the same building, apartment 7B, became a place of solitude when I craved a peaceful setting after a long day at work finishing my chores in my brother's apartment. At the Dawson's residence, I experienced a mother and father's love since I lost my father at the age of four on April 4, 1951. Mrs. E. Dawson, whom I nicknamed as Mums, and Dad a.k.a. Pops, we called each other every weekend up to 2019. He's now ninety-nine years young, a bond which developed since 1965.

On several occasions, their daughter invited me to accompany her to social gatherings such as birthday parties, christenings, and matinee movies. Although we live in the same building, my brother insisted I return home before midnight. Isn't midnight the time people begin to show up at parties?

His excuse was being an "African Orthodox priest" under the leadership of Bishop Wilkey at St. Mary's African Orthodox Church located at 118th Street, Lenox Avenue, New York. He needed adequate rest to perform his duties effectively the following day of worship, Sunday.

On several occasions upon returning to my apartment as I opened the door, the tenants on the third floor as well as below our apartment would be entertained by a loud noise from our apartment as the vacuum cleaner/floor polisher which was placed behind the door would fall to the ground.

My brother would meet me in the hallway as I walked toward my bedroom, which I shared with my seven-year-old niece, questioning, "Where did you come from?" As if he didn't give me permission to accompany my adopted parent's daughter to the function.

If this man wasn't crazy, I wonder what you would call a person operating with that type of mentality and behavior. At times, my neighbors would question me, stating, "Why does Father behaves like that?" I couldn't give them an answer for fear of reprisal because he always threatens to have me placed on the next place leaving "Island Wide" a.k.a. John F. Kennedy International Airport.

December 26th, 1967 the Dawson's was blessed with their first grandchild, unfortunately, born out of wedlock. Upon hearing the news of the baby, my brother stated that I like visiting the Dawson's because I wanted to become like their daughter.

A friend of their daughter who was on leave from the US Army happened to be visiting while I was at their apartment. He asked the Dawsons if they would allow him to go out on a date with me. They informed him that my brother was very strict; therefore, he should write my brother requesting his permission which Henry did.

Finally, I felt appreciated by my brother, oh yes! One could never tell what tricks my brother was up to or what his next move would be. Well, I was granted permission to go to an evening movie. Henry showed up nicely dressed. My brother invited him to sit at the end of the sofa. His daughter was told to sit next to her father while I sat on the opposite end of the sofa. After a half an hour of interrogation, we left for the movie. I returned around 8:00 p.m.

Henry made a second visit to my brother's home because of his interest in developing a relationship with me. Permission was granted to arrive around 6:30 p.m. Seating was arranged as usual. However, around 7:00 p.m., my brother got up from the sofa, walked toward his bedroom, and returned wearing his pajamas.

Henry stood up as he headed towards the door, I ask my brother's permission to accompany him to the elevator.

He responded, "Okay, kiddo."

Which I interpreted that it was okay. Well, upon my return five seconds later, Vincent struck me on my back with a broken baseball bat, stating, "You think you're a woman? Get out of my house now."

I started to cry as I question him "why did he strike me?"

He responded, "Don't question me. Get the hell out of my apartment now." He proceeded to pull my clothes off the hangers and placing them in black garbage bags.

It was a cold day in December, snowing. I cried uncontrollably. I couldn't understand why he was acting in such an irrational way. I didn't know what to do or where to go.

Eventually, I summed up enough courage to call one of my childhood girlfriends from Harlem Christian Mission Church (an affiliation of the Christian Mission Church in Bedford-Stuyvesant). Her grandfather, Mr. Fagan, who was a friend of the family, informed me to board a taxi to his house where he rented rooms. Upon my arrival from 103rd Street, Amsterdam Avenue to 122nd Street, Lenox Avenue, Harlem, Mr. Fagan and his granddaughter, Glenda, welcome me with open arms as they assisted me to my new digs with my possessions.

A few hours later, I was led to my new digs. It was a small bedroom with a bed and commode. I shared the kitchen and bathroom with two other families—a lady from St. Croix and a gentleman living down the corridor from my apartment.

What an experience. I was forced to accept at the tender age of nineteen years old in this new country. With the Christian foundation laid by my mum and my faith in God, I quickly settled down. My landlord, Mr. Fagan, prepared my meals daily at the end of the week. I paid him $6.78. During the week and on Sundays, I worship with him and his granddaughter at the Eben-Ezer Christian Mission Church.

I wrote to Mum explaining what had transpired between my brother Vincent and me. He had already filled her head with lies as well as his friends and family members stating that I think I'm grown. Therefore, I left his house and move to Harlem.

Really? I learn to trust God in the midst of my troublesome circumstances despite of the surmounting storms I encountered. Exercising my Christian faith and background, I learn to trust God knowing that he would eventually grant me deliverance. 1 Peter 4:12–13 (KJV) says,

> Beloved, think it not strange concerning the fiery trial which is to try you as though some strange thing happen unto you. But rejoice in as much as ye partakers of Christ suffering; that when His Glory shall be revealed, ye may be glad also with exceeding joy.

Reflecting back to one of Mum's favorite phrases, "A lie walks around barefoot, but the truth delays because it needs time to dress." Meaning, a lie spreads like wildfire; however, the truth will eventually take precedence. Mum express great concern about my new residence, especially around the area of 125th Street where marijuana was sold in the open. And it was common to see young men hanging out in groups, some appeared to be sitting in midair. Remember it was the '60s, the year of the "flower children, groupies, free love, etc." I survived with God's help and protection. Psalm 23:4 (KJV) states, "Yea though I walk through the valley of the shadow of death, I fear no evil for thou art with me; thy rod and thy staff they comfort me." Psalm 23:6 states, "Surely goodness and mercy shall follow me all the days of my life."

On two occasions while traveling on the NYC mass transit train to work, my brother Vincent and I happened to ride in the same car. He approached me stating that Mum was extremely worried about my safety living in Harlem on my own. Mum and I bonded like sisters; therefore, I understood her concern for my safety. Before I migrated to the USA, we were inseparable. We shared stories about her past and spent quality time together. I left Barbados because she wanted me to accomplish my goal and profession. She reluctantly agreed to let me leave the island. We miss one another's company. We were very close.

However, there was a line of demarcation. She never allowed us to forget (respect). In other words, watch what you say in her presence. She encouraged me to return to my brother's apartment because she had spoken to him concerning what had transpired between us. Being an obedient daughter exercising my faith trusting God, he would see me through my storm.

On several occasions, my brother Vincent encouraged me to return to his premise. I adamantly told him only on under certain conditions I would consider returning to my old residence providing that he agreed to certain stipulations I listed namely: (*a*) he must respect me, (*b*) stop belittling me, (*c*) stop abusing me both physical and mentally, and (*d*) if I'm invited out to a function, please allow me to return by 1:00 a.m. instead of midnight.

He agreed wholeheartedly; therefore, I reluctantly return. As the saying goes, "A tiger doesn't change his spots." Another phrase people use is, "A dog that sucks eggs will always suck eggs." The first month upon my return, everything seems as if my brother had changed. Surprise?

"If a dog bites you, it's the dog's fault. But if you get bitten the second time around, it's your fault." Well, well, within a short space of time, Reverend Vincent resumed to his nasty unorthodox ways such as:

1. Ordering me to wash his laundry in the bathtub, especially his white shirts which the Asian laundry's poor cleaning resulted in an ashy gray underarms
2. Cleaning his clerical garments
3. Polishing and vacuuming the house

The only reprieved I received is when my body was monthly cycling. He stated that I was unclean; therefore, I shouldn't touch his clerical garments. What a reprieve. I was delighted to be unclean. What a breather.

One day, my brother, my niece, and I went to JFK International Airport to see a friend off. On our way back to the car park, Reverend Vincent couldn't recall where the car was parked. Instead of taking responsibility for his actions, he insisted that I should have paid attention. We walked around for over an hour as he ridiculed me stating I was no help to him.

Being domesticated (e.g., cooking, baking, sewing, engaging in arts and crafts), I boarded the number 7 bus to Fourteenth Street, the shopping area, and purchased over fifteen yards of upholstery fabrics from Ash Hill Fabrics Store, making my first set of slip covers for a sofa and love seat which were badly worn around the arm rest of the furniture. I also bought rugs and curtains, sprucing up the apartment which added an ambiance to the apartment setting.

When my brother's friends visited him, he was very proud of my sewing techniques, stating, "One day, you'll make a nice wife to a good man." He was overprotective of me. Was it because he enjoyed me being his slave or did he really have my best interest at heart?

Yes! I was attractive, long hair, nicely built, and always dresses conservatively. I was the center of attraction when I entered a room. He couldn't stand the attention drawn to me—a nice Christian girl (old school). When I notified the family of his erratic behavior toward me, I kindly asked them to show leniency because at the end of the day, I lived at his residence.

On one occasion, I seasoned a fowl which I thought was a chicken (remember in the island back in those days, we only prepared chickens for a meal). I prepared the meat as usual, deep frying it as I laid the table for us to partake.

As my brother took his first bite, he exclaimed, "What the you've done?"

I said, "What do you mean?"

He responded, "This is a fowl. You should have boiled it for hours. Look, this meat is like a leather."

I felt humiliated like Eva Gabor when she tried making toast. She always burns up the toast.

Once, I cooked a lettuce. He was so infuriated yelling, "Who do you know cooks lettuce?"

In Barbados, most lettuce grows with long leaves like stems. They're never curled up in a ball like cabbage, the reason why I cook the vegetable. I couldn't do anything right to please Reverend Vincent.

I reached a point in my life being despondent that I considered contemplating suicidal thoughts. I wondered how it would affect Mum; therefore, I prayed and prayed seeking God's guidance and deliverance from my tormented brother. I aspired to be strong asking God for the wisdom of Solomon. Being who Solomon was, he could have inquired of God for material things; however, he knew he needed wisdom and knowledge to guide his nation.

I left my brother's church and joined Grace Methodist Church located on 104th Street off Amsterdam Avenue, New York. Reverend Tatem, the officiating minister from the Bahamas, West Indies, was instrumental in consulting and encouraging me to be strong because God promises to never leave us or forsake us. I loved singing the hymns of praise. They reminded me of the hymns I sang as a youngster growing up in the West Indies. God omnipotent and God omnipresent, he delivered Daniel from the lion's den. He delivered the three Hebrew boys; therefore, he would deliver me. I believe God would change things soon.

A few months later, a friend of my brother known as Aunt Whilamena introduced me to my late husband (died on April 22, 2013, after forty-four years of marriage), Adin Elnathan Walkes. I prayed and asked God for a husband who wouldn't be abusive, a nonsmoker, nondrinker, and a Christian man who would love me unconditionally. God gave me just what I requested. I forgot to ask for a romantic lover (smile). Hello, you can't get everything. Just be thankful.

Our first date took place on January 28, 1968. He couldn't take his eyes off me. We met at 103rd Street, Broadway subway local number 1 train station. We walked to my brother's apartment which was located one block away. As a matter of fact, he could see from his kitchen window people coming and leaving the 103rd Street train station.

My brother was consistently sat next to my future husband as he had directed my former date, Henry, months before. After half an hour of interrogations, we left the apartment on our way to Carvel ice cream store. We needed something sweet to break the tension, returning to the playground at 103rd Street. On our return to the building grounds, we sat on the park bench communicating, getting to know each other.

On our second date, I introduced my fiancé (Adin) to my adopted parents, Mr. and Mrs. Dawson, and their family. They bonded well. Mr. Dawson and my fiancé had several things in common, especially playing cards and dominoes as a pastime sport. Mum and Pops gave my husband an invitation stating that he was welcome to visit at any time.

On February 14, 1968, Valentine's Day, my fiancé presented me with a gold chain with a locket and a beautiful card stating that he loves me. The words I longed to hear. Doesn't everyone want to be loved?

My brother stated that my fiancé wasn't welcome at his apartment because he didn't know if he had good intentions. However, my adopted parents stated, "He could visit at any time."

I wrote to my birth mother (Florence) in Barbados expressing my love for my fiancé. What a small world. Mum knew his father, Elder Robert Walkes, a preacher at the Church of God. She gave me her blessings. I invited her to New York for her approval of my relationship to Adin since my fiancé stated that he didn't want a drawn-out relationship. He wanted to get married before the end of the year 1968.

On June 16, 1968, he stated that he wanted to get engaged. All the things I longed for was finally coming to pass. I asked my fiancé why June 16. It's because he was born on June 7 and my birthday was on June 9. We compromised and settled for June 16.

Reverend Tatem officiated at our engagement party, which was held at my brother's residence, thanks to Mum. Vincent told my fiancé I wasn't domesticated (can't cook, iron clothing, nor take care of an apartment). I was humiliated.

My fiancée requested I visit his brother's premises where he lived. Surprisingly, he requested I press a shirt for him. I gladly accepted the challenge. On one occasion, I left work early and invited him to my brother's residence for dinner where he watch me prepare a sumptuous meal (steak and onions).

My fiancé told me he had something to tell me; however, he delayed the information each time I inquired about it. "Surprise, surprise," as Gomer Pyle's TV character used to say, I learned what the hidden secret was when we appeared at the registrar office to fill out the application for the marriage license. I immediately notice he recorded the year of his birth. I was deceived because he appeared to be younger than his age. My brother Reverend Vincent upon meeting him on the first visit stated that he looked like between twenty-five to thirty years old. It dampened my euthanasian.

Well, it all depends on whether the person took care of their body, yes! He delivered although I was a bit skeptical thinking because of his age I would be confronted with a problem later in life. But looking at the overall picture, we must be grateful for everything. We set a date for October 5, 1968 to be joined in a holy matrimony. He was a good Christian man, loving father, and a good husband. The wedding was well attended by family and friends. My brother Vincent was the father giver reluctantly, but Mum insisted. I relocated to Brooklyn, New York.

Our union produced two lovely children—1 girl Charleen followed by a boy Charles 4 years later whom my mother assisted in raising until they started primary school.

I continued to work at Bear Stearns Company up to 1972. Eventually moving on to Burlington Industries in 1345 Avenue where I worked for Greige Fabrics until they relocated to Greensboro, North Carolina, in 1973. All employees were given three weeks' pay and were dismissed. I asked my brother Reverend Vincent whether BUG (Brooklyn Union Gas Company) had job openings. He stated no.

One day when one of his friends, Mr. Sealy (a Salesman from (BUG) Brooklyn Union Gas Company was visiting Reverend Vincent home, I happened to be present. I asked him whether BUG was hiring.

He said, "Why don't you apply?"

Which I did. I received a call for an interview in December 1973. Three weeks after I was laid off from Burlington Industries, I passed the test for work employment at (BUG) Brooklyn Union Gas Company. However, I was informed that January 14, 1974 would be my starting date at Brooklyn Union Gas Company. I was excited to know that I was hired by a company with job security. The Bible states, "Blessed is everyone who fears the Lord who walks in his way. When you eat the labor of your hands, you shall be happy and it shall be well with you."

Approximately, one month working in Data Processing Department, a young lady from the West Indies was hired because a job opening became readily available. I was happy to know that I had a company since at times I felt left out. However, sometimes you don't realize how happy you are until Satan shows his ugly head as my Mum stated. She became envious of my clothing to the point that she made ugly remarks along with threats.

After a few weeks of the nonsense, I wrote a registration letter to the director of data processing operations, Mr. Smartie, stating, "In the year of our Lord January 1974, I was approached by one of my coworkers who deem it fit to make my life a living hell resulting in an uncomfortable situation. As a result, I'm unable to function 100 percent of my ability. Regrettably, I'm resigning from my job."

Mr. Smartie summoned me to his office forthwith, stating that this type of writing skill could be benefited by the company in the Correspondence Department. The following week, I was pro-moted to the Correspondence Department including a $45 raise in pay. This action created a volcanic eruption in the Data Processing Department. Unknown to me, some of my coworkers wanted to get out of the department; however, they were informed that they could apply after a year. Arbitration letters started to grow rapidly because of my promotion. To quell and satisfy my coworkers who had tenure and wanted out of data processing, the company open positions pro-motions as Clerk 1 status to the Credit and Collection Department to avoid litigation between management and the local union. Shortly afterwards, I receive another promotion to work in the district offices as a Teller which I gladly accepted.

August 7th 1969 our first child was born sick. Her sickness motivated me to return to the classroom pursuing a course in Pediatrics' and Geriatric Care at the Metropolitan School of Pediatrics and Geriatrics in Manhattan, New York. The course provided with the necessary tools I needed to care for our baby and the elderly. I received a certificate from Metropolitan School of Infant and Geriatric Care in 1969.

God is an on-time God. My nursing skills for geriatrics services was utilized again in 1999 when my husband tried lighting the boiler at our home by placing his hand near the burner—bad move. He sustained third degree burns on his hands and face. After one week of hospitalization at Staten Island Hospital, a visiting nurse administered TLC (tender, loving care to his wounds). As I observed how she wrapped and applied medication, she told me that I seem interested. Why don't I try while she observed me.

Upon the second trial, she said the family have no need for her services. I was qualified to administer the same services which I gladly accepted.

During my tenure at Brooklyn Union Gas Company, the crossroads of life at times were quite unfavorable. Through it all, I survived the mountains, valleys, and detours. Working as a teller in the district offices, I met people from all walks of life with varying personalities, cultures, and issues as they paid their gas bills, establish gas accounts, and disputing bills.

The first serious problem I encountered was with a customer whose gas service was terminated. He lived on Long Island renting a house in Brooklyn with tenants whose gas service was terminated. In order to restore the gas service, reconnection fees, a security deposit, and settlement of the bill were required. The customer paid the reconnection fees and the bill but reluctantly refused to pay the security deposit, which was one of the main requirements to restore the gas service. He walked out of the building annoyed and returned tossing the deposit receipt on my desk.

I hurriedly wrote a receipt for the security deposit of $300.00 without inquiring whether he had made a payment. At the close of the day as I balanced my bills and receipts against the checks, I was short of $300.00. The head teller and I discovered that the particular customer account wasn't fully paid. Several calls to his home was ignored. As a result, I was informed that it was my responsibility to cover the charges out of pocket. I prayed earnestly to God seeking guidance how I should handle the situation. I wrote to Life Study Fellowship, a group of prayer warriors who encouraged me to be strong, knowing God would work a miracle on my behalf.

The customer's wife threatened to sue the gas company for harassment because they had satisfied full payment of the required bill. *Lies, lies*. Both the customer and I was offered to take a *polygraph test*.

The husband reluctantly refused. I passed the test twice which cleared my name. I questioned the technician who performed the test as to why I was given the test. He stated that the company thought I took the money. How ludicrous.

A few days later, the customer mailed the deposit receipt. Thank God for answering my prayer. As a result, I was placed on a six-month probation. At the end of six months, I received a promotion as a Customer Service Interviewer, interviewing customers with various problems such as:

- Paying their bills
- Making deferred payments to satisfy outstanding bills
- Interviewing customers whose gas services was interrupted for various reasons
- Emergency services, etc.

I enjoyed my job meeting with the customers on a one-on-one basis.

One of my coworkers by the name of Dueblo, whose advances I spurred, threatened to kidnap me one night after leaving classes at Medgar Evers College as I walked to my car. He threatened to have an affair with me whenever the opportunity present itself even if it was in the undertaker parlor, if I died before him. I filed numerous complaints which was dismissed by the management. After seven years of harassment, I had enough of the nonsense. Therefore, I requested a transfer to another branch office which was granted while I was on vacation.

To my surprise when I returned to work as I approached my station, who should I see sitting at the new station smiling, stating, "You think you got away from me?"

I felt humiliated thinking what should I do next. Let's face it, delay isn't denial. God's ways aren't our ways, and his time isn't our timing.

One day while I was absent from the office, Dueblo threatened the supervisor who complained to the security and claims department. They escorted him out of the building. Unknown to him, the various district offices where he worked, both management personnel and coworkers who had encounters with him, had complied a stack of complaints against him. Therefore, he was suspended with recommendation for dismissal. Yes! He had exhausted everyone's patience.

Satan looks after his own. Yes, he does. Well, Dueblo landed a job with the Department of Corrections with a licensed to carry a gun. Mercy, Lord. His job was less than a quarter of a mile from my work place.

During my lunch hour, we would cross paths. I asked, "Dear God, why?"

I refused to live in fear. In 2 Timothy 1:7 (KJV), it states, "For God did not give us a spirit of fear but of love, peace, and a sound mind." I stand on God's word. I later learned Dueblo had an altercation with one of the prisoners sustaining medical treatment. He retired on disability. I haven't seen or heard from him since over the last thirty years. I'll share with you a few scenarios of sexual harassment which I encountered back in the 1980s.

SEXUAL HARASSMENT

Case 1

I've been passed over for promotions time and time again; however, I held on to my morals and values. One day, one of the egotistical office director challenged me, stating that he could get any piece of he desired.

Really?

I responded that this is one piece of you wouldn't get although I had a permanent spot at the branch office because of tenure. He found it necessary to bounce me from office to office as a punishment for refusing to succumb to his sexual advances.

Again, a woman's scorn.

Case 2

Another branch office supervisor, who we referred to as Mr. Bossie, informed me that I could advance far in the corporation. However, "I would be required to give a little to get much."

Really?

He further stated, "Variety is the spice of life. Don't wait until you get old and regret you didn't reach the highest heights at the top of the mountain."

Well! Well! I responded to the supervisor, "When my husband sleeps with your wife, I'll consider having an affair with you."

I knew I looked good, but why did they continue to pursue me? Only God knows.

A group of my neighbors back in the early 1970s told me that three men on my block gambled to determine which one of them would be the first to be intimate with me. My God, my God.

Case 3

An elderly district office manager, Mr. Blue, requested me to drive him to a location during working hours, which I obliged because it presented the opportunity to take care of my business. I was told that he would call me on my Nextel when he was ready to return to the office.

Upon completion of his chores, he suggested we stop off at a famous restaurant in Bedford-Stuyvesant a.k.a. Stuyvesant Heights for lunch. The restaurant was owned and operated by three colored sisters. The name of the restaurant is called McDonalds. I questioned why they were using the same name as the chain restaurant McDonalds. He told gave me the history about the restaurant.

No problem. He ordered a martini. I ordered a Sprite soda. He was annoyed that I ordered a soft drink. He said to drop him off at his apartment at Downtown Brooklyn as he made his advances while I was driving. Again, a woman's scorn.

On one occasion, a customer visited my station stating that he was awaiting for the gas service to be restored. He had taken a day off from work, and no one showed up. I immediately called the dispatchers at the main office requesting for a favor. They told that me they could accommodate me. Therefore, I proceeded to issue an order for the same-day services.

My manager, Mr. Blue, sat at his desk listening to the conversation between the customer and I. He found it necessary to suspend me stating that I'm well aware that there's no same-day services order.

I explained to Mr. Blue about the customer's dilemma. He wasn't interested in my explanation. Therefore, he suspended me ordering me to leave the company premises forthwith.

Case 4

One day, my son who was fourteen years of age visited me at my workplace. As I looked into his face, I sensed that he could benefit from a few removal of moles in his face. Therefore, I called our dermatologist whose office was approximately five minutes away from my workplace requesting an appointment ASAP for my son. She instructed me to come right away, well!

I informed the female assistant supervisor, Ms. Burnell, where I was going on my evening break. I further stated that if I overstayed my time, I would gladly make it up for it. The supervisor who was at odds with me inquired about my absence. His assistant supervisor stated she didn't know where I was.

Really?

My fair-weather coworkers kept quiet as I was threatened and harassed upon returning to work. Basically, the dermatologist, Dr. Green, forgot I was at work as we stayed in the waiting room for over ten minutes without acknowledgment. I exited the room reminding her I was on break. She conducted and removed the moles forthwith.

However, upon returning to work, my supervisor, Lydon, summoned me to his office threatening to suspend me with recommendation for dismissal, adding that I could only return if the union won arbitration on my behalf. I requested to speak to my union delegate who demanded to see my impeccable records which failed to reveal any reason for suspension since I was always on time, my performance appraisal scored high, I was a team player, and always volunteering to assist whenever called upon. She (the union delegate) questioned Lydon as to what was the reason for the hostility which he never had an answer.

God showed up in my favor. I wasn't suspended. I later learned that the supervisor's friend, Ms. Gober, had influenced him to relieve me of my duties in that department. Haters! But if God would be for us, who can be against us? Time wouldn't allow me to talk of the injustice some of my coworkers as well as myself encountered at the hands of prejudice managers working at my workplace.

Case 5

My first encounter working with a seductive female supervisor, Ms. Tee my namesake in the district office. The female workers were harassed verbally while the male workers were seduced as she found it necessary to press her voluptuous breast on their back as she bends over their backs explaining whatever with her fingers meandering through their hair as they sat at their stations.

I tried to win her love by loaning her my clothes, sometimes selling her clothing whenever an emergency impromptu party invite surfaced. As the saying goes, "Money can't buy love. Love comes from the heart." In this world, there's a difference between love and pretense. As human beings, we all want to gain the affection of people. However, at some point in our lives, we must face facts that the Bible clearly illustrates on Palm Sunday, people in the New Testament hailed King Jesus. That same week on Good Friday, they said to Pontius Pilate to crucify him and give them Barabbas (the thief). When I consider all the good that Jesus did, it wasn't enough to stop the evil crowd from turning their backs on him. Then who am I?

When customers visited the office to pay bills or to resolve an issue with the gas company, 99 percent of the time, they mistook me as the supervisor which irked Ms. Tee. Could it be the professional way I dress and conduct myself?

At times after the customer left my station, she would shout out my name summoning me to her office and immediately demanding whether the customer solicited my assistance instead of speaking to her directly.

I think only the customers could answer these questions, right?

One day, Reverend Youngbland representing one of his parishioners solicited my help in filling out a questionnaire in order to receive funds from New York City under a program called HEAP (Home Energy Assistant Program). At one point, we reached a section on the application requesting personal information which he wasn't privy to. I advised him to bring the application to the person he was representing explaining the various areas needed to be completed in order for the application to be processed.

Ms. Tee, the supervisor, overheard the conversation and proceeded to the information desk which was the first stop when a customer expressed an interest to speak to a customer service representative or to a supervisor. She informed the clerk at the information desk when the Reverend return the following day, direct him to her office.

Following the instructions of Ms. Tee, the Reverend was directed to the supervisor's office. As the Reverend proceeded to Ms. Tee's office, he acknowledged me at which point Ms. Tee came out of her office, stating, "This isn't a social gathering." She demanded me to report to her office after summoning up my customer transaction.

Upon entering the office, I greeted the Reverend. Ms. Tee instructed me to sit down accusing me of denying the Reverend assistance on behalf of the person he was representing. I tried to explain what had transpired.

She snapped. "Stop." She requested to hear the Reverend's version of the story wherein he indicated that I assisted him as much as I could. However, additional information was required needed which could only be provided by the person he was representing. She replied, directing her focus toward me, she'll see who's the *liar*.

The Reverend got up out of his seat, thanking both of us for our concern as he exited her office. She instructed me the dialogue between her and me wasn't finish as she released me to return to my station.

The following week one evening as I was about to exit the door at 5:00 p.m., she yelled, "Walksie" referring to me. "Is your monthly cycle on?"

I emphatically told her that she was out of order. She went on to say that I had left a bloody spot under the toilet seat. This woman was incredible. Her plans was to engage me in a confrontation which would result in insubordination resulting in suspension from my workplace.

If this wasn't harassment, what is it?

In another occasion, she called a district office manager, Mr. Sierre Leona, stating that I reminded her so much of her mother. Informing him, she overheard me telling a coworker, "I would kick his."

I immediately asked her why was she being so resentful toward me.

She responded, "Don't worry about it, Walksie" as she patted me on the shoulder.

One day while walking by my station, she pulled on my blouse stating, "I need to wear my clothes with flare."

I responded, "Don't worry about it."

She further stated, "I have blotchy skin. Why don't I use beeswax to even out the color of my skin? Because when a man takes off a woman's clothing, he doesn't want to see blotches."

I informed her that my husband of twenty-two years doesn't complain about skin.

She continued with her insults stating that my husband and I live double lives. He works at night, and I work at days. I need to quit my job and meet him at the door when he arrives wearing a sexy negligee.

I informed her that "as a jockey, my horse always crosses the finish line."

She laughed stating, "We got a hot mama over here."

Again, I asked her why she displays such dislike toward me. She responded that I have a lot of similarities of her mother; therefore, she can't stand me.

Refusing to give up on becoming her friend, one day, she was given an impromptu invitation to an affair by a Con Edison worker. She asked to borrow a dress. Well, I immediately left the office and drove home bringing her a brand-new dress with a $500.00 price tag. She became very infuriated; however, she wore the dress. Surely, I thought to myself that she would like me. Oh no, the drama continued.

Our company's, Brooklyn Union Gas's, public relations (PR) department always ended up with excess tickets to various affairs due to cancellations. Therefore, supervisors would offer the tickets to the workers. On one occasion, I accepted two tickets for my husband and me. The event was held at the Fleur De Lis's catering hall. Well, I was decked out wearing a tailored dress with a beaded neckline. Surprisingly while dancing, Ms. Tee approached me as she tugged on my beads. I prayed to God that she would let go without snapping the beads. My praise was answered. "What an evil woman."

Finally, I complained to a union delegate filing a harassment suit. Her response was that I barely make it to work on time. I'm confused, and she doesn't know what I'm talking about.

Really?

I submitted a request to be transferred to the head office. She stated that I could be suspended before the transfer is approved. Well, it was approved, not before she called the district office supervisor, Mr. Fallon, narrating all the negativity and lies against me.

My first day at work in the main office, I received a hearty welcome from my coworkers. During the course of the day, my new supervisor summoned me to his office laying down all the ground rules, the job function, and highlighting everyone in his department gets along with each other. I told him to "give me the opportunity to prove myself."

At the end of the month during my Performance Appraisal (PA), he gave me high scores as he stated how happy he was to have me on board. I thanked him for observing my work ethics and for judging me based on his observation rather than on hearsay.

I also received an award known as Employee of the Quarter. The award is given to an employee who receives high scores in their ability to do as follows:

1. Exhibits high performance
2. Meets and exceeds productivity
3. Meets workload requirements
4. Plans and uses time effectively
5. Superior planning and time management skills
6. Promotes productivity and safety among coworkers
7. Very good at planning and time management
8. Including work ethics, attendance, and customer satisfaction

Employee of the Quarter award was the beginning of the many awards given to me. There's also Incentive Award in first and second quarter of 1985, People's Choice Award in 1987, and Special Recognition Award in 1992. In addition to numerous letters of compliments from customers.

In the Bible, Joseph's brothers who was jealous of him tried to get rid of him, but God placed him in Egypt to save their lives during the famine. Ms. Tee tried her utmost best to destroy me, but God highlighted the qualities in me, expelling all the negativity which proceeded my transfer from the district offices to the main office headquarters of (BUG) Brooklyn Union Gas Company.

The awards entitled the recipient and a guest to a lavish lunch at a prestigious restaurant where a plaque is presented, summing up with the remainder of the day off.

Within a year, I received a promotion entitled Collection Controller. Isn't God good?

As I previously pointed out, there's issues in every department. I was assigned to the Legal Department, of which I was the only female. Of course, I encountered resentment because the male counterparts felt like they would have to clean up their vocabulary, which made them feel uneasy.

One day, I found a box on my desk with the words written, "Smith and Weston." I had no idea what it meant. I was later told that it's an ammunition gun company. Also, remarks were made such as "how many more n———s are coming into this department?"

Being a Christian and believer with great faith, I knew God had my back. Therefore, no weapon formed against me would prosper, and every tongue that rises up against me would be condemned.

Case 6

I joined Brooklyn Union Gas Christmas Choir group December 1974 because I love to sing also prior to relocating to New York as a little girl I sang at Festivities both at Primary school and Sunday School, matriculating to the Adult Choir choral group, During the month of December Brooklyn Union Chorus group sang at the Main office entertaining gas company customers, employees as well as visiting School children who usually participate at times especially when a song was familiar to them (Rudolph the Red nose reindeer). The chorus group also sang at various locations such as Nursing Homes, as well as Brooklyn Union Gas aka National Grid district field locations.

At the end of our tour the Christmas Choir Group was treated by the company with a sumptuous lunch at Marco Polo, an exclusive restaurant in the neighborhood. While attending a dinner in our honor, dinner was delayed when I receive a call from a family member who was in the area stating they would wait around in their car to give me a ride home. I brought it to the attention of a Supervisor who stated "no problem", he could join us. I relayed the message to the family member who later joined me at my table. The gown mistress MB became rather infuriated inquiring why the family was present, dropping humiliating remarks which I ignored. A few days later while passing her in the hallway at work, she said to me "someone told her they were planning to put 2 bullets in the back of my head." I question why would someone make such a dreadful remark, she implied because the Christmas Dinner is in honor of Brooklyn Christmas Choir only. I told her why was she so concern, is it over a plate of food which I had permission from the Supervisor for my family member to join me. Rumors spread all over the building about the plate of food. I couldn't believe my coworkers could entertain such hatred to the point of wanting to take my life. Fortunately, I receive a call to Grand Jury, I brought it to the attention of the District Attorney well as the my Union president who advised me she would conduct and investigation and get back to me. Well! Well! to my surprise she informed me Marte Beber made the remark jokingly. The following day Marte Beber boss summoned me to his office, informing me Marte Beber is his secretary she was joking, don't take this any further. Out of fear of being further harassed and humiliated on the job I decided it would be in my best interest to forego any further claims. I know if I had verbalize such threats it wouldn't have been swept under the carpet it would only be a matter of time before the company got rid of me. It was very hurtful knowing I didn't even get an apology, but God allow me to continue working 18 years later with a comfortable retirement package. I enjoyed my job, but it was a struggle keeping my head above the water, however, I survive to God be the Glory.

John 15:18–19 (NKJV) states,

> If the world hates you, it hated me before it hated you. If ye were of the world, the world would love his own, but because we're not of the world, but because I have chosen you out of the world therefore, the world hates you.

A few months later, I was assigned to the Multifamily Department, which I loved. The new position entitled me to handle a variety of accounts and interacting with various account managers representing high profile companies, corporations, businesses, hospitals, churches, and airport accounts. At the beginning of the month, I was assigned approximately over 150 clients owing Brooklyn Union Gas Company monies ranging from $3000.00–$9000.00 in uncollectable gas bills.

My job function consisted of meeting with various account managers, setting up Deferred Payment Agreements (DPAs) to satisfy the outstanding debts.

I became a proficient successful Collection Controller receiving numerous awards and several customer's satisfactory letters.

In December 2003, I accepted an early retirement at the age of fifty-five years of age to care for my mum who had relocated back to Barbados and was experiencing ill-health due to diabetes. This dreadful disease weakened her body as she advanced in age going into her nineties.

Unfortunately, my life took a negative turn. In November 2004 while visiting my mum, I was diagnosed with breast cancer stage 350.5 metastasizing. It shook my world. No one in my family was diagnosed with cancer. I prayed to God while questioning myself what cause this deadly disease to invade my body.

My focus was diverted from my mum's health to my health, seeking the best medical treatment I could afford because I wanted to live and raise my two children and enjoy my husband, who immediately called to schedule an appointment with my doctor in New York.

Upon my return to New York, my worst fear was confirmed at Long Island College Hospital (LICH) where I underwent my first of many surgeries. Post-surgery follow-up indicated that the cancer was spreading rapidly. Therefore, there was nothing more my doctor could do for me.

I responded to Dr. Holpkamp "God is in charge", he stated "he hopes so".

I hurriedly left the doctor's office as my husband and I hailed a taxi to take us to our home. My husband ask me "what was the doctor's diagnosis". Upon hearing the word cancer, he froze like a statue.

Well, I prayed like never before, calling every preacher I knew because the Bible states, "Where two or three are gathered together in his name, he's in the mist of them." I poured out my heart to God, asking him for healing and forgiveness, for anything I had said or done amiss. I refused to accept defeat robbing me of precious memories and the love of my family and friends I've acquired over the years. I was confident God would answer my prayer on my behalf.

Well! God is an on-time God. He may not come when we want him, but he surely comes on time. God answered my prayer, the prayers of my family and faithful saints, eliminating all doubts, fears, and negativity which consistently invaded my thoughts.

One of my coworkers, Josey, referred me to Memorial Sloan Kettering Cancer Center where I had the privilege of speaking with Dr. Jeannie Petreck (oncologist) who informed me what documents was required to perform surgery. I met the hospital requirements providing the necessary documents scheduling an appointment for surgery.

On January 25, 2005, while sitting in the waiting room, I was approached by a nun who stated that she was looking for a patient by the name of Mrs. Ernestine Walkes. I informed her that I was the person she was looking for. She ask me if she could pray for me. I responded "Yes".

Honey, she surprised me. She prayed like a "Pentecostal worshipper," asking God to touch my body from the crown of my head to the sole of my feet and requesting that he would only allow the doctors to perform the necessary surgery without any exploratory advancements. She also prayed for God to send his Angels to sterilized all the equipment being used (during surgery) and finally, granting me a speedy recovery. With that prayer, I knew God sent her to comfort me and to show me he would be with me throughout the surgery, restoring me back to good health according to his will.

Major surgery was performed at Memorial Sloan Kettering Cancer Center by Dr. Jeannie Petreck (deceased) in 2005. Isn't God good? He allowed her to save my life before he called her home from labor to rest. A few months after my surgery unfortunately Dr., Jeanne Petreck succumbed to an untimely death April 13, 2005 being struck by a motor vehicle while crossing 2nd Avenue and 64th street on her way back to her office. Dr Petreck and I formed a bond during the short space of time January 2005, when I was introduced to her prior to surgery. She was a people's person, warm, gentle, kind and compassionate, an attentive listener who treated her patients like family. A woman of her caliber exhibit humility saving over 4,0000 women lives, because she love her job, her patients wellness and health both prior to surgery and recovery was her main concern.

Dr. Jeanne Petreck was a pioneer in her field being a Professor at Cornell University School of Medicine. Upon learning of her sudden death I loss it. How could this happen to such a lovely caring human being who saved Over 4,000 women lives especially mine. Psalms 116:15 Precious in the sight of the Lord is the death of His Saints KJV

Thank God for technology, however, with her skillful hands, God given wisdom and faith thank God fifteen years later I'm enjoying opulent health, discarding Dr. Holkept statement "there's nothing more he could do", since the Breast Cancer was 3.50 metastasizing rapidly, but God the great physician spared my life. With sincere gratitude a year after recovery I became a Peer Navigator, at SUNY Downstate Medical Center, working with patients undergoing treatment both with Radiation and chemotherapy bringing them hope, building up their faith knowing there's a light at the end off the tunnel. Yes! life is a journey because sickness try to shorten our stay here on earth, we must learn to fight the good fight. Someone once said "we're what we eat" therefore, its of vital importance we exercise, eat a balance diet, take time out to rest, be greatfull for the mountains and valleys in our lives knowing someone out there is in a worst situation than you're experiencing. Someone once said "there's no testimony without a test".

Yes! We serve an awesome God.

I am humble and thankful to say fifteen years later, I'm happy to be found in the land of the living enjoying opulent health. Thank

God for good friends, caring family, preachers worldwide, and Memorial Sloan Kettering Cancer Center.

Isn't God awesome? Yes! He is.

I received six months of chemotherapy followed by six months of radiation.

Chemotherapy is highly recommended; however, the cells which the medicine intended to target, causes the good cells to become damaged. In most cases, chemotherapy damages the heart, collapsing the veins and also impairing the respiratory system. When death comes knocking at your door, any suggestions offered to you for a cure, you tend to gladly accept with the hope that it would prolong one's life. My veins collapsed resulting in additional surgery to install a "port" under the skin connected to a major vein in my chest, allowing the medical team easy access to my blood whenever necessary.

To my surprise after the first treatment of chemotherapy the following morning, I noticed my long locks of hair on my pillow. I cried uncontrollably. All the hair on my body hair disappeared. My body looked like a newborn baby. I became hysterical. I wasn't prepared for the shocked I encountered. I lost my appetite, feeling of weakness invaded my body to the point that I couldn't stand for more than a few minutes. The metallic taste of the medicine lingered in my mouth for months, the smell of food made me feel sick, and my skin turned a shade darker—all the signs I experienced was a reflection of someone awaiting Simon Peter's call. Especially after I received the second treatment of "radiation" which eradicated the skin off my chest as the rawness of my flesh left a foul odor, which was cured by applying a 12 x 6 DuraDerm plaster patch.

Day by day, I experienced a miracle on my body as the raw flesh began to turn pink and blotchy (which is an indication of the healing process). A few weeks later, I observed little dots like pinholes appearing on my chest. Gradually, my natural skin color began to blend in, praise God. My hands and feet displayed dark brown spots. My fingernails and toenails continued to grow out at a rapid pace.

I thank God for Memorial Sloan Kettering Cancer Center and their staff.

I thank God for who he is. He's not the man that would lie.

I thank God for his unmerited favor toward me and all those calling upon him.

I thank God for praying partners.

I thank God for a strong faith.

I thank God for my family support.

God is an awesome God. He didn't have to do it, but he did. He's a God of second chances.

The medical staff at Memorial Sloan Kettering Cancer Center is remarkable There are like family taking the patients' health seriously. At the end of my treatment, I received three months follow-up, six months follow-up, ending with yearly follow-up which ended in 2010.

During the year 2010, I was introduced to a plastic surgeon at MSKCC who promise to enhance my femininity. Yes! He did. He's as gifted with the scalpel as Michael Jordan in basketball. Dr. B. Mehara (plastic surgeon) was a miracle worker. I can attest to his creativity and handiworks of God.

Well! Twelve years later, my hands continue to display a few brown spots—a result of the chemotherapy medicine. Gradually, the pigmentation of my skin began to shed returning to my natural skin color. Viewing pictures of before and after, I looked completely different, which was obvious to many people. I knew I was awaiting a call from Simon Peter. Unknown to me, God was bragging about me. Like Job in the Bible, I console myself saying, "Though he slay me, I [Ernestine] would yet praise him because my sickness wasn't unto death but that God would be glorified." Can he do it? Yes, he can.

One day, I visited my regular beautician. She inquired what type of treatment I was looking to be done. Immediately, I assumed she didn't recognized who I was. When I told her who I was, she said she knows the voice, but it's not the person she thinks it is. I told her I had been diagnosed with cancer as I removed the cap off my head and told her that yes, I'm one of her favorite customers.

She fled to the back of the store stating, "Don't do this to me."

I was so insulted as I returned to the car crying. I consoled myself knowing that it was her way of reacting to me knowing that she used to complain that my hair was so thick and long. The time she took to work on my hair, she could finish two customers. Well, that's life.

Now that my chest was healed and I could wear loose clothing for a longer period of time, I decided to visit my church where my family and I worshipped over the past twenty-five years. To my surprise, most of the parishioners scattered like cockroaches when the light was turned on. I felt hurt, humiliated, and disappointed; therefore, I hurriedly exited the church.

One would think I was inflicted with a contagious disease. My church friends scorned me. The only telephone calls I received was from two of the oldest church mothers. Subsequently, my pastor, M. B., visited me once as he interrogated me, questioning me, "Did I lose a breast?" More unnecessary humiliation. Question, if I did, what was he going to do with the information? It's amazing human beings both educated and uneducated at times can be very insensitive towards another individual feelings.

I decided to return to church after my skin color and my facial structure was returning to normalcy. During my stay at home, I worshipped by way of the media such as Trinity Broadcasting Network (TBN) and Word Network, which continued to nourish my body, soul, and spirit.

One Sunday, the Pastor's nephew during one of his sermons talked about sickness amongst the saints of God, he pointed out cancer isn't contagious. Everyone has cancer cells. What causes the cells to mutate and metastasize, no one knows. The congregation being now educated had a change of heart toward me. Feeling comfortable, they began to greet me with a handshake especially during "meet and greet." Finally, as time went by, my hair began to grow all over my body. I began to look more and more like myself again which made the church folks feel more comfortable around me.

Question: Where in the Bible Jesus scorned or avoided the sick? In Matthew 9:12 (KJV), which states, "Those who are well have no need of a physician but those who are sick."

Like Peter in the Bible when he bid Jesus to come to him as he walked on the water, everything seemed to go well for him until

Peter took his eyes off Jesus and began to sink. But Jesus stretch forth his hand and saved Peter. Well, Jesus is the great miracle worker who stretches forth his hand, healing my body completely.

Isn't God wonderful? Yes! He is.

Isaiah 43:2 (KJV) states,

> When you pass through the waters, I will be with you; and through the rivers, they shall not overwhelm you; when you walk through fire you shall not be burned and the flame shall not consume you.

Therefore, holding God Almighty to his word knowing that he's not a man that would lie, I believe he would heal me, and he did. Wherever I go, people think I look extremely good for my age. They don't believe that I'm a senior, and most of all, they can't believe that I had been inflicted with that dreadful disease.

I praise God every day for waking me up and keeping me in my right mind. I thank him for faithful praying partners. I look back and thank him for what he's done in my life and what he's about to do in the future. I thank him for the great faith because faith without work is dead.

When the doctor prescribed the medication for us, by means of faith, we use the medication because we believe it will cure our ailment; therefore, it's contingent upon us to exercise our faith.

He didn't have to do it, but he did. Thank God for a second chance in life.

My children and my husband were my biggest supporters. My husband, who was an introvert, never talked about my sickness neither did he questioned me about my feelings. His world was shaken by my sickness. I knew he loved me unconditionally. I watched as his health began to spiral downhill due to my illness. He was afraid of losing me.

A few weeks prior to his death, he underwent an operation at Mt. Sinai Hospital to relieve the pressure of his spinal cord being affected by arthritis. A small insertion was done on his neck. He was forced to use a catheter for five days until the follow-up. During the short period of time, the catheter became infected resulting in his groin being enlarged to the size of an orange, resulting in inflammation oozing from the surgical area.

My husband was readmitted to a local hospital where he suffered a massive heart attack during his sleep on April 22, 2013. The night before he passed away the children and I visited him, we played cards while watching a ball game. Little did we know that it would be the last time we would be enjoying his company as a family.

My children lost a good father. I lost a good husband, a provider, a man of God with an impeccable character, and an honest man who not only profess to be a Christian but was genuine in all his ways—a no-nonsense person.

During my husband stay at the hospital surprisingly no one from our church visited him. KJV John 21:16 Jesus ask Peter "lovest thou me?". Feed my sheep. Adding insult to injury no one from my church call our home or visited him when he was discharged.

Shortly after my illness, his health began to progressively grow worse. He developed Parkinson's disease, dementia, and coronary disease resulting in seven stent operations as he was diagnosed with 98 percent blockage in his heart.

It's amazing how people change. Christian followers place your trust in the Lord, mankind will fail you. My entire family were pillars of our former church over 25 years. I recently found a Thank You card from my former Pastor thanking our family for our support and devoted interest in the church addressing the various needs financially before they were officially brought to the congregation attention. However, when my husband was unable to attend church no one called or visited our home.

Whether or not we attended church services our tithes, offerings as well as pledges were always submitted in a timely manner. At times we fool ourselves believing people have our best interest at heart only to be disappointed.

Could it be my husband and I over evaluated our relationship with the Pastor's family? My family labor of love spread across the ocean to the (UK) United Kingdom where the first family was entertained by family members, yet it took 3 months after my husband's death before the Pastor place a call to our residence. However, he found it convenient to call stating "if God would lead me back to my former place of worship the church would be bless"

Really? Did he miss the large contributions for the upkeep of the church. Romans 12:3 (KJV) states "Don't think yourself more highly than you ought to think, but to think soberly, according as God hath dealt to every man the measure of faith".

Isn't God wonderful, Yes! He is.

Isaiah 43:2 KJV states "When you pass through the waters I will be with you; and through the rivers, they shall not overwhelm you; when you walk through fire you shall not be burned, and the flame shall not consume you."

Therefore, holding God Almighty to His word, knowing that He's not man that He should lie I believe He would heal me, and He did. Where ever I goes people think I look extremely good for my age, they don't believe I'm a Senior, and most of all they can't believe I had been afflicted with that dreadful disease.

I praise God every day for waking me up and keeping me in my right mind.

I thank Him for faithful praying partners.

I look back and thank Him for what He's done in my life and what He's about to do in the future.

I thank Him for great Faith, because faith without works is dead NKJV…James 2:14–26, when the doctor prescribes medication for us, by means of faith we use the medication because we believe it will cure our ailment; therefore, its contingent upon us to exercise our faith.

He didn't have to do it, but He did. Thank God for a second chance in life.

Being a motivational speaker, I'm confronted by people from all walks of life. These people are amazed by my radiant, youthful appearance and positive outlook. Yes, cancer had my body, but mentally speaking, I didn't have cancer. My body was going through a transition while God was bragging about me. He promises to never leave us or forsake us, admonishing us to call upon him. He's closer to us than the breath in our nostrils.

Psalm 34:6 (KJV) states, "This poor man cried, and the Lord heard him, and saved him out of all his troubles." Yes! God answers prayers. The Bible states that "Job" was afflicted with sore boils from the sole of his feet unto the crown of his head (Job 2:7). He was deserted by his friends. His wife questioned him, "Dost thou still retain thine integrity? Curse God and die."

The medical staff at Memorial Sloan Kettering Cancer Center is remarkable, having their patients' best interest at heart. Following my diagnosis, I received three months follow-up then six months follow-up, graduating to yearly follow-up which ended in 2010.

I spoke to my oncologist, Dr. Tari King, who replaced Dr. Jeannie Petreck. She informed me that I had passed the five-year grace period; therefore, she was assigning me to Ms. Rodriguez, a physician assistant (PA). She was one of the most caring individuals you could ever meet, delivering impeccable care toward me.

During the month of September 2010, I met with an incredible plastic surgeon at MSKCC—Dr. B. M. He's a magician. He promises and he delivers. All I can say is, "Oh my God." Besides being extremely handsome, there's magic in his hands.

Upon meeting me for the first time, he told me, "I will make you feel feminine again," and he did.

He's as gifted with the scalpel as Michael Jordan is gifted with the basketball. Over the years, I've read various plaques at the beauty parlor; however, the words on one of the plaques resonates in my memory, it states, "I'm a beautician, not a magician" because most woman brings a picture of a particular hairstyle, expecting the beautician to deliver the same or similar hairstyle whether or not it compliments their facial structure.

As a New York license cosmetologist, I was taught to study the facial structure since faces come in various shapes (e.g., oval, round, square, and heart shape). Therefore, every hairstyle isn't suitable for everyone's face although an oval face usually compliments various hairstyles. However, beauticians do their utmost best to satisfy their customers. Again, I give credit to the person/people who deserves to be complimented.

Dr. B. Mehara at Memorial Sloan Kettering Cancer Center is a miracle worker. May God continues to bless his hands as he enjoys making women feminine again due to the individual being unhappy with their appearance. I can attest to Dr. B. Mehara's creativity and handiworks. I recommended him to everyone when doctors asked me where I had my plastic surgery. I boldly informed them at MSKCC under the professional guidance of Dr. B. Mehara. So far, I've had six successful surgeries. God is awesome.

My body went through a transition while God was bragging about me. He promises to never leaves us or forsakes us, admonishing us to call upon him for he careth for us.

Yes! God hears and answers prayer. It may not always be what we want to hear, but trust me, he'll answer our prayers. Like Job in the Bible who was afflicted with sore boils from the sole of his feet unto the crown of his head Job 2: 7, he was deserted by his friends, his wife question him "Dost thou still retain thine integrity? Curse God and die. In Job 13:15, Job said, "Though he slay me, yet will I trust in him." God bless the latter end of Job more than his beginning (Job 42:10).

I celebrate the gift of life everyday despite the roadblocks, detours, valleys, and mountains. All these components make us stronger individuals because there's no testimony without a test.

Bishop Eula Campbell (deceased) was instrumental in building my faith during my diagnoses and recovery. She reached out to several prayer warriors on my behalf for God to heal me. One of the faithful prayer warriors I've yet to meet is Evangelist Brown. What a phenomenal prayer warrior who intercede long hours praying, wrestling with God at which point through prayer and intercession God blessed me with the gift of the "Holy Ghost" with the evidence of speaking in tongues, as in the Gospel of Acts 2:1–4.

And when the day of Pentecost has fully come, they were all with one accord in one place. And suddenly, they were sitting and appeared unto them cloven tongues like as fire. It sat upon each of them, and they were filled with the Holy Ghost and began to speak with other tongues as the Spirit gave them utterance. I asked God for a passage of scripture indicating that I would be healed. As I opened the Bible, my focus was directed to Psalm 30:1–2, 5, which states,

> I will extol thee, O Lord, for thou hast lifted me up, and hast not made my foes to triumph over me. Oh Lord I cried unto thee, and thou hast healed me. Weeping may endure for a night but joy cometh in the morning.

Believing God's word, I felt relax realizing he had my back. Surely, I would recover from the dreadful disease. Well, I believe God's word; therefore, I felt relax realizing God surely have my back. Day by day, I experienced a miracle on my body as the raw flesh on my chest began to turn pink. A few weeks later, I observed a tiny gray-like pinholes on my chest as the skin gradually started to gain back to its natural color.

Praise God.

My diagnoses of Cancer had a devastating effect on my husband (Adin) he was an introvert very quiet in nature. I recalled when Dr. Holtkamp first gave me the diagnoses he stood at attention like" Lord Nelson" statue.

His health spiral downhill due to my illness, he was afraid of losing me. Shortly after my diagnosis Adin develop coronary problems, the first stent was installed 2004 subsequently the last stent was installed 2012.

My children, Charleen and Charles, were my biggest fans, giving me words of encouragement stating my bald head makes me look younger. My mum stated one day that I looked like a boy with a short haircut. I felt hurt, but I smiled because I didn't want to hurt her feelings.

After two years of recovery, I decided to volunteer my services at SUNY Downstate Medical Center and Kings County Hospital in the cancer unit. I became a breast cancer advocate, motivational speaker, and patient navigator. I joined several cancer organizations namely as follows:

1. American Cancer Society, rising to chaplain under the directorship of Jean Campbell
2. Member of the National Breast Cancer Coalition (NBCC) under the leadership of Fran Visco
3. Peer navigator at SUNY Downstate Medical Center, consulting breast cancer patients, newly diagnosed as well as those who have reoccurrences and gathering data, which was faxed to Washington, D.C., headquarters
4. Share Cancer Organization, NYC.

CANCER

It's a malignant growth (tumor) which is the result of cells for unknown reasons grow out of control.

Base on scientific evidence our bodies consist of approximately 37 trillion cells which is replace daily by new cells, broken down into 2 categories

(a) Red blood cells live for a shorter time usually 4 months

(a) white blood cells which lives basically for about year

(b) The number of cells in a human body varies from person to person base on the structure of our bodies.

Cancer cells due to unknown reasons metastasize, outliving normal cells ultimately developing into abnormal cells meanderings into various parts of the body attacking the organs, lymph nodes and vessels, where they grow. We're also mindful of the fact cancer cells can also be pass on by means of DNA.

Although cancer is the leading cause of death in the United States, millions of people who was diagnosed with some form of cancer is alive today due to early diagnosis and treatment. With today's technology in the case of Breast Cancer, the removal of the breast (mastectomy) isn't necessary. Tumors are targeted and removed followed by Chemotherapy and Radiation.

My body developing Breast Cancer was beyond my comprehension since I'm the last of 8 siblings and was the first one in the family to be diagnosed with Cancer. Since the age of 40 years old I consistently subjected my body to a yearly dose of Radiation by means of a Mammogram.

In most cases a physician recommends a diagnostic mammogram when abnormality (lumps), nipple discharge tenderness, pain is detected. An X-ray of the breast is conducted by a technician who specializes in breast imaging, during which time pictures of the breast of the individual is taken and examined to identify the status of the abnormality. Diagnostic mammograms are non-invasive. When a woman's ovaries are removed the possibility of developing Breast Cancer or Ovarian Cancer is nil. Unfortunately, while vacationing in the West Indies December 2003, I was diagnosed with Stage 3.50 Breast Cancer? what a scare. I ask the question, "why Lord?"

Reflecting on Job in the Bible, a prophet a man who feared God and shunned evil, lived a blameless and upright life. Satan question God stating "Doth Job fear God for nought, hast thou made a hedge about him, his house all his inheritance". Put forth thine hand and he will curse thee to thine face. God said to Satan, all that he hath is in thine power, only upon himself put not forth thine hand. power what had he done to deserve the humiliation and punishment he succumb, God was proving a point to Satan. Job lost almost all of his cherish possessions to the point his friends accused him, his wife told him to curse God and die. I admire his stamina because he trusted God enduring life conflict,

Job prayed for his friends, as a result God blessed the latter end of Job more than his beginning KJV 42:12.

However, my motto is "if He brings you to it, guarantee He will bring you through it". "There's no testimony without a test".

One year after I retired from National Grid, accepting an early retirement package in order to care for my elderly ailing mother (Florence Waterman) 96 years old, whose body was ravished with Diabetes.

Gomer Pyle on television uses to say surprise, surprise, surprise Yes! What a life-threatening surprise. In life we don't know what awaits us around the corner. Cancer shook my world, life is like a deck of cards at times you're fortunate to be dealt a good hand, sometimes you're rather unfortune therefore, you try your utmost best accepting the consequences and move on. Someone once said when life offers lemons make lemonade its refreshing drink on the rocks.

It's interesting to know, both women and men get Breast Cancer, of which men developing Breast Cancer is a smaller percentage, than women. Her2- Human epidermal growth factor receptor 2- negative of which I was a recipient (He) most common type. Hr+ hormone receptor positive

Ultimately, in order to enjoy a better quality of life it's in our best interest to change our diet and lifestyle implementing proteins, carbohydrates, fats, water and exercise. Exercise is important in order to maintain a suitable body weight base on our height and frame.

Foods should consist of proteins such as poultry, meats, seafood cheeses, eggs, milk and water (8) glasses daily. Vegetables should include fiber and beans. Food such as cured meats, franks, ham, contains a high percentage of sodium which cancer patients should avoid.

Multivitamins and medication should be taken as prescribed

Follow-up doctor visit is very important, in order to maintain a good quality of life.

Patients are educated in areas of health care, finance, exercise, and their spirits are nurtured building their hope and faith. We are what we eat. By eating healthy, we're nurturing our bodies which will enable us to enjoy a better quality of life. When a person is diagnosed with cancer, the first signal that resonates in their brain is death. I encourage my counterparts that there's life beyond cancer. The doctor's diagnoses are based on education in the medical field; however, Jesus the great physician has the final word.

Life's a journey. Surely one day, it will come to an end; therefore, it's important to enjoy every moment. Live life to its fullest. Wake up every day with a positive attitude and a positive frame of mind, giving thanks to be on the wake-up list.

I volunteered my services at YWCA Brooklyn cancer care division along with one of their representatives, Ms. M. Laguerre.

Our job function consists of reviewing a list of cancer patients from the YWCA file. Contact was generally made over the telephone and by way of correspondence. Based on customers' needs, we prioritize visits to the customers residences. Upon visitation, customers are informed of the various options available to them both from a medical standpoint as well as by means of referrals to various agencies and organizations who readily volunteer their services, lessening the burden of cancer victims and their families.

Obtaining the needed support motivates them to live. Changing one's diet is of vital importance because we're what we eat. Proper nutrition is an integral factor to restoration of one's health. Exercise keeps the body flexible.

We thank God for a wake-up call. Some people experienced a sudden death. Someone said, "Life's a journey" one day it will come to an end, therefore, its incumbent to enjoy life to its fullest.

Wake up praising God, eat, drink plenty of water, exercise, and enjoy life with a positive frame of mind. Volunteer your services in the community. There's lots of lonely people in the world.

Volunteers are needed at public schools (PS). I mentored a middle school at PS under the auspices of Junior Achievement Program, teaching kids how to develop self-esteem, role playing for jobs interviews as well as how to prepare for the job market, speaking properly, dressing appropriately, respecting themselves as well as others, always exhibiting professional mannerism and budgeting their finances, and most importantly, graduating from high school and excelling to a higher standard of education advancing to college because the sky is the limit. Volunteers are needed at community centers, hospitals, nursing homes, etc. Each one teaches one; let's make this world a better place. Share the love in living Heaven on Earth.

Over the years, I've learned to appreciate the experiences of life, the knowledge I've accumulated, and the precious gift of a second chance in life as a survivor living in a spiritual life. I've had the privilege to travel all over the world, mainly the West Indies, North and South America, Asia, Europe, the Mediterranean, Israel, Australia, New Zealand, and Russia. These are places I read about as a child. Never had I envisioned that after the diagnosis of cancer, I would have been able to travel around the globe. Isn't God good? I'll never forget after the confirmation of my diagnosis in New York by LICH, Dr. Holtkamp emphatically told me that there's nothing more he could do for me. I have to get my priorities together. I cried out to God, and he heard me.

I considered myself a successful professional business woman who have overcame all odds, thanking and glorifying God for his grace and unmerited favor toward me. The good book states, "No good thing will he withhold from them that walk uprightly." He's the God of impossibilities we only need to be patient placing our trust in God. Delay isn't denial. Keeping a positive attitude has been a contributing factor to my wellness.

I aligned myself with individuals who have my best interest at heart. Praying without ceasing gives me strength day by day, learning to forgive, closing the book on the past to excel as we go forth into the future. The airlines cut down on baggage; we also can.

We're told that Jesus folded up his clothing and leaving it behind. If we are his followers emulating him, we too must close the book and move on. Philippians 3:13–14 says, "Forgetting those things which are behind and reaching forth unto those things which are before, I press toward the mark for the prize of the high calling of God in Christ Jesus."

INSENSITIVITY

My beloved brother Archpriest Primate (African Orthodox Church) who lives in Canada, reaching the pinnacle of his career governing numerous African Orthodox churches worldwide, forgot the same God who granted him the elevation he usurps could easily be taken away from him. The Bible states that promotion doesn't come from the East or West, but it comes from God.

During a visit to New York, a family get together ensued addressing ways to increase monthly contributions toward the upkeep of our mother (Florence Waterman deceased). Five of her eight children signed an agreement stating how much they could contribute on monthly basis which would lessen the pressure I encountered knowing I shoulder most of the burden of the bills. As we took turns explaining how much we would contribute, when big brother's opportunity came around, he emphatically stated that he has nothing to give. He's a pensioner. He being the firstborn, he knows he's entitled to her assets whenever she passes away.

A blowup among the siblings ensued focusing on me since Mum "willed the house to me."

He reiterated his statement, "You, you should be dead."

I couldn't believe what I was hearing. I responded, "What did you say?"

He reintegrated, "You should be dead." He immediately left the room to join his wife and family members who were occupying another room. Eventually, everyone began to disperse leaving me and my one brother in the room. Immediately, his wife, first lady Isa, approached me swinging like a boxer as she became very verbal with her remarks.

One of my sister-in-law's gripped her arms from behind preventing her from striking me knowing I was recovering from breast surgery. My brother never apologizes for his behavior over the years neither did he apologize for his chaotic behavior toward me as a teenager when I lived at his residence for over three years.

A year ago, when he was diagnosed with cancer and was approached by two of our brothers questioning him of the inhumane treatment suffered by their baby sister, he stated that any wrong he committed, God will forgive him.

I failed to see the humility exhibited by my brother, a man of the cloth leading the flock. My comfort and consolation is that "may God have mercy on his soul." He's right in stating that God will forgive us of any sins we committed once we confess our sins; however, why should we play victim, spreading animosity amongst future generations instead of simply and humbly saying, "I'm sorry"?

The Bible states that David was a murderer, but he seeks God's forgiveness. God forgave him. God stated that David was a man after his own heart. Abraham lied to the pharaoh stating that his wife was his sister, fearing he could be killed in Egypt. God forgave him because of his obedience to him. As a result, God promise to bless his seed as the sand upon the seashore. Time wouldn't permit me to cover God's blessing upon his people. Christ came to serve. As Christians, our ways and actions should be a reflection of Christ Jesus.

Humility

> For it was not an enemy that reproach me;
> then I could have borne it: neither was it he that
> hated me that did magnify himself against me;
> then would I have hid myself from him. But it
> was a thou a man my equal, my guide and my
> acquaintance. (Ps. 55:12–13, KJV)

> For the Lord seeth not as man seeth; for
> man look at the outward appearance, but the
> Lord looketh on the heart. (1 Sam. 16:7)

He delivered me from my strong enemy, and from them which hated me: for they were too strong for me.

Therefore hath the Lord recompensed me according to my righteousness, according to the cleanness of my hands in His eyesight. (Ps. 18:17, 24)

CARING AND NURTURING

One day Mum told me we need to talk, well! we both sat me down as I listen to her attentively, she stated you have reached the age of adolescent, therefore, there were certain valuable lessons you need to know as you journey through life maintaining my integrity at all times as a young lady; exhibiting Godly characteristics, morals, and values because a person is judge by their character and the company they associate themselves with."

The topics she focus on was as follows:

Respect- first you must respect your self in order for others to respect you
Dignity- maintain your dignity at all times, think before you speak, spoken words cannot be erase
Manners- Always exhibit mannerism
Show kindness and empathy when its warranted
Humility-you cant please everyone, however when you've done your best pray asking God for guidance. Pride comes before a fall.

I love my Mum dearly it's amazing how certain words people says plays on your mind. Being an attentive listener I tried to make her proud of me at all times. I was the baby of the family, her little Princess. Don't get it twisted the day you step out of bounds, the rod of correction was administered forthwith. She was an avid reader, who taught her siblings the importance of reading broadening their vocabulary since society judges you by the way you speak.

In the 20th century if parents would devote time teaching their children to be respectful, taking pride in themselves especially when communicating instead of using profanity as a means of expression, love would supersede disparity. Vulgarity seems to be the norm in some households resulting in children learning profanity before they're taught their ABC's its so sad; also parents and grandparents are competing wearing either the same type of attire or similar. It's becoming the norm observing young ladies attending church, lacking dress code (wearing the same type of attire they wear to the club). Young men wearing their pants beneath their buttocks, however, this type of inappropriate attire is unacceptable in the court of law. Parents its time to set rules and guidelines, children reciprocate in the manner they're taught. It's never too late to correct the wrong.

A poem I learn in primary school states "Drive the nail a right boy, hit it on the head. Strike with all your might boy, while the iron red. Though you stumble off boy, never be down cast, strike, and strike gain boy, you'll succeed at last… Standing at the foot boy, gazing at the sky, how will you reach up there boy if you never try." Someone once said "I'll rather attempt to do something and fail, than to do nothing and succeed." Let's get a grip, we as grandparents been there, done that, step back let's lead by example.

Children are a gift from God, as parents we have a responsibility to teach, guard and protect them, until they reach the age of maturity as stipulated by the law. However, if we fail to execute our responsibilities not only will God Almighty hold us accountable; but the LAW will execute judgement which may not be in our best interest. Parents, Guardians lets step up to the plate. Amen.

TRIBUTE

It would be amiss if I didn't pay a tribute to my third eldest brother who was instrumental in my successful journey. Unfortunately, he passed away on August 2, 2017, at the age of eighty-four years old succumbing to myeloma cancer. During the early 1950s, my brother Rudolf became the father figure and role model for me and three siblings since our father died in April 1950 (HBP and stroke).

We (my younger brother and two nephews) obeyed his instructions emulating him as he delegated orders and assumed the role of a father. Mum never question his authority which he carried out expeditiously. Rudolf assigned homework which included the British pounds, mathematical tables since the West Indies were operating under the British system. My brother was very passionate about education in regard to his younger siblings and two nephews.

I recalled Rudolph teaching our five-year-old nephew and eight-year-old me the alphabet and mathematical tables as listed on the back of the notebooks, in addition to the 2× tables up to the 12× tables. Let's not forget the pounds and shillings tables up to twenty-one shillings a guinea. What a waste the currency used in those days (pounds, shilling, and pence) are now obsolete.

My brother like my mum (Florence) never spared the rod. I was the recipient of some of those lashes. I recalled screaming after a good whipping, "Go ahead when you're done killing me. You'll bury me." I say emphatically, his interest in my academic achievement is a contributing factor to my successful journey in life.

In retrospect, looking back, I'm grateful for his involvement in my life. Growing up, Rudolf was a very intelligent and ardent student with a quest for knowledge. In elementary school, he earned a distinction award called Vestry which is a scholarship entitling the recipient to advance to a secondary school.

In 1955, he migrated to London to join our sister in pursuit of advancing his education pursuing a better quality of life. He worked as an engineer with the British railroad moving on to employers working in the corporate finance. Rudolph was a lodge member being firstly a member of the Rosecuitions then later a member of Freemasons, reaching the level of "Grand Master." During the month of April 2007, Rudolf was made "Freeman of the City of London." This honor was first granted to King Edward the Second in 1319. He also displayed a mark of exemplary character and behavior. His only regret was that our mum (Florence) who passed away wasn't alive to celebrate his accomplishments and achievements.

A few years after my husband of forty-five years passed away from a coronary heart disease, I entered into a relationship with a Christian man, who I also believe was a religious man. What a surprise, I quickly learned that there's a difference between a Christian and being religious. Two years into the relationship, I questioned him, "Where is the relationship going?"

His response was shocking to me. He said, "How do I threat you? How is my actions towards you, my dear? I'm not ready to get married. I want someone to take care of me when I get old."

Really? I responded, "If marriage wasn't in your future, why shower me with gifts including jewelry, stating this isn't what you're looking for, but I hope you'll like it."

He introduced me to his family and his friends.

Sisters, listen carefully to me. When a man wants you to his wife, he introduces you as his fiancée/his queen. When he only wants to use you, he introduces you as his friend. Don't try to buy his love or settle while he treats you as an option.

Your value is more than what he's offering. Let's face it. Everyone who enters your life isn't part of your destiny.

Yes! I say let him go. It hurts but love yourself and let him go. People must accept you for who you are. Ask yourself, "What am I expecting to get out of this relationship?" Are you looking for a serious relationship or are you only interested on one thing?

Move on and learn to say goodbye because time lost can't be regain. God closes one door, and he opens another. Don't hold on to a loser.

Sisters, if you're looking to settle down, be up front with your partner after a few dates and place your cards on the table. After six months into a relationship, if he keeps the relationship as a secret, get out of it—run. If he introduces you as a friend after a year, he's playing you. That's all he'll settle for; he's not looking to make you his wife. If he introduces you as his queen/his lady, he's interested in you. More likely, you're the one he wants to spend the rest of his life with.

Don't try changing your partner, he'll lie stating he promise, that's just for the moment, although if he truly interested in you and value the relationship he will change. If you really want to prove his love, get him angry. His response dictates if he's the right person for you. Based on the answers he gives you, it's contingent upon your part to decide.

As Steve Harvey states, relationships are based on three Ps—purpose, protection, and possession. If a man cares for you, it's because there's a purpose. He'll always protect you because he values you.

As women we must learn men language. Most of the time, they're on point. Don't keep your head down in the sand. We live in a real world. During our lifetime, we're susceptible to roadblocks and bums as we navigate through life. It's not easy. Saints and sinners seek an easy way to manipulate others with their cunning techniques.

In this world, we will meet narcissistic men. They tell you what you want to hear. You'll also meet genuine men who will accept you for who you are and treat you like a queen. Narcissistic men are usually egotistic (full of themselves) and talks about how good looking they are, describes their assets, materialistic—it's all about them. They think they're God's gift to women. They're full of themselves, egotistical.

Players are exactly what is described as a player. Players are usually involved with several women. Why? This is their mode of operation. Usually, they don't keep appointments. Why? If one partner isn't available to accommodate the player, impromptu, he goes down the list calling up one of his other ladies (options). A player tells you what you want to hear as he questions you, asking, "What are you doing? Get dress" as he invites you to go for lunch, to a movie, or for a ride. When a player is busted, instead of giving a reason for their infidelity when the subject is brought to the forum, the response is, "Let's move on." No accountability is given for their actions.

Ladies, love yourself. Stop waiting for someone to take you out to dinner, on a boat ride, a bus ride, a walk in the park, or to the museum. If your girlfriends aren't available, sums up the courage and go solo. You'll be surprise during your journey you may meet your queen/king. Enjoy your life. Time lost can't be retrieved.

Don't get it twisted. Some sisters are also players. They exhibit the same cunning habits as the opposite sex, sometimes worst. Men tend to become highly offended when they find out they're being played. Weak-minded men, who for lack of control, resort to physical harm toward their partner, sometimes resulting in death. Society accepts the fact that it's okay for a man to cheat; however, it's unacceptable for a woman to cheat. Perfect example is found on John 8:4 (KJV) which says, "They say unto him, Master, this woman was taken in adultery, in the very act." When a woman cheats, it's disgraceful. She's regarded as the lowest human being.

Senior citizens a.k.a. recycle teenagers looking for companionship, be very careful. Identify what you really want out of a relationship. The same rules apply when you were a young lady on the market. This statement goes for men also.

Loneliness is a "killer." However, it's better to be lonely and comfortable than to get involved with "a wolf in sheep's clothing."

The Bible states, "Seek ye first the Kingdom of God and his righteousness and all things will be added unto you." As human beings especially as we advance in age, our patience grows short. We must learn to wait. At the beginning of the relationship, our partners seem to have all the attributes our hearts desires; therefore, we rush off and get married. Three to six months into the marriage, you find yourself stuck with a parasite, becoming a caretaker, health aide with a partner draining your energy. Suddenly, all the luxuries which attracted you to them abruptly stop. Why?

Let's keep it real. Most seniors over the years fail to plan for their future. "Therefore, if you fail to plan, you plan to fail." The reason why the cash flow stops it's because they're broke, broke, broke.

In the twilight of the remaining years, whatever time is left on the journey, they're looking for someone to (sponge off) support them. The only thing they have to offer is memories. Yes, I say emphatically memories. Seniors, if you're looking for more, you'll get more than you bargain for, such as old age and diseases accompanied by various types of pain which is part of the package deal. I encourage all senior citizens to "look before you leap"—one of my mother's phrases. Don't fall for looks and a smooth talker. Seniors, continue the gift of gab until death.

They're out their Seniors, unless his 401K and W2 tax statement reflects a good income. The Bible states, "He will keep us in perfect peace whose mind is stayed on thee" (KJV).

Growing up in the West Indies, I use to hear the old ladies say, "When you have an itch, drink lemonade or grapefruit juice. It's better over the rocks."

As I advance in age, I view each day as an adventure plan by God, not my will but his will be done in my life. I'm on this earth for a reason.

I'm glad for the foundation laid by my mother (Florence) and my brother Rudolf, both deceased. My mentors, guardians, and friends who were instrumental in my development and success in life. I embrace the pitfall and roadblocks which made me a stronger person. Cancer ravished my body. The challenge taught me humility as my faith developed, soaring on a higher plane. I quickly learned to be thankful for whatever state or frame of mind I'm experiencing. I embrace it knowing that if God brought me to it, he has the power to bring me through it. I thank God for his unmerited favor toward me, my family, and friends. Writing this book brings closure which needed to be address over fifty years. I hope this book will inspire, educate, and bring a source of understanding and comfort to people of ages as we journey through life.

Reflecting of the journey God placed on Joseph prepared him for the position of president of Egypt. There's no testimony without a test. When I reflect on the words of Shakespeare, "Friends, Romans, countrymen, loan me your ear," we should seek God's divine guidance in everything we do. Not our will but his will, will be done.

REFERENCES

Excerpts from KJV, Steve Harvey, Shakespeare.

(ACS) American Cancer Society, Lindsay Waterman

ABOUT THE AUTHOR

Ernestine Walkes was born on June 9, 1947, the last of the eight children—six boys, two girls—of Westerman and Florence Waterman. She migrated to the USA from Barbados on May 25, 1965, following her dream of pursuing a nursing career.

Ernestine met her husband, Adin Walkes, through a friend, Wilhermina Alford. Being attracted to each other from the onset, they got engaged on June 16, 1968, followed by the holy matrimony on October 5, 1965. The union produced two children—one girl and one boy.

In having a quest for knowledge, she pursued her studies at St. Frances College and Medgar Evers College where she graduated BSc Bachelor of Science 1988. International Theological Seminary of California, Master of Theology 2006, determine to fulfill her childhood dream as a Hair Stylist, she studied at Hair Design Institute, becoming a NYS License as a Cosmetologist 1995.

She believes in giving back to society therefore, she volunteered her services with several organizations "Meals on Heels, through Heights and Hills, Junior Acheivement, Cancer organizations Share, (NBCC) National Breast Cancer Coalition, (ACS) American Cancer Society where she became a Peer Navigator, excelling to Chaplain of American Cancer Society August 2008.

CPSIA information can be obtained
at www.ICGtesting.com
Printed in the USA
FSHW010712021020
74301FS